D1016896

CONGRESS-PERSON

Troll Associates

CONGRESS-PERSON

by Louis Sabin

Illustrated by Bob Dole

Troll Associates

Library of Congress Cataloging in Publication Data

Sabin, Louis.
    Congressperson.

    Summary: Discusses how senators and representatives
are elected and how they go about making the laws of
our country.
        1. Legislators—United States—Juvenile literature.
2. United States. Congress—Juvenile literature.
[1. Legislators. 2. United States. Congress]
I. Dole, Bob, ill. II. Title.
JK1064.S23   1985   328.73'073   84-2651
ISBN 0-8167-0266-7 (lib. bdg.)
ISBN 0-8167-0267-5 (pbk.)

On September 17, 1787, members of the Constitutional Convention gathered in Independence Hall in Philadelphia. They were there to sign the Constitution of the United States of America.

The Constitution established a strong national government—one that is divided into three equal branches. The judicial branch explains the laws. The executive branch enforces the laws. And the legislative branch actually makes the laws.

The legislative branch of the federal government is called the Congress. Congress is made up of two houses, the Senate and the House of Representatives. The Senate's 100 members—two from each state in the Union—are elected by the voters to serve terms of six years. There is no limit to the number of terms they may be reelected to.

Senators must be at least thirty years old, must be United States citizens for at least nine years, and must be legal residents of the state that elects them. One third of the members of the Senate are elected every two years. This means that two thirds of the senators are not new members at any given time. So the Senate is sometimes called a continuous body.

The Vice President of the United States serves as president of the Senate. But the Vice President cannot vote on matters before the Senate unless the voting is tied. Then the Vice President may choose to cast the deciding vote.

Any senator may place a bill before the Senate for its consideration. A bill is a proposal for a law. But it does not become a law unless it is approved by both houses of Congress and is signed by the President. Senators may propose bills on any subject except money. Money bills must start in the House of Representatives.

There are 435 members in the House of Representatives. The number of representatives from each state is determined by the population of the state. Each member of the House represents nearly 500,000 people. That is the population of an average congressional district. Each representative is elected to a two-year term by the voters in his or her district. There is no limit to the number of times a representative may be reelected.

Representatives must be at least twenty-five years of age, citizens of the United States for at least seven years, and residents of the state in which they are elected. Members may propose bills on any subject, but the main power of the House of Representatives is to originate money bills. Of course, after the House passes a money bill, it must still be passed by the Senate and signed by the President before it becomes law.

13

Many bills that come before the two houses of Congress are voted on along party lines. The two leading political parties in the United States are the Republican and the Democratic parties. In each house of Congress, whichever party has more members is called the majority party. The party with fewer members is called the minority party.

Before any bills are voted on in Congress, they are worked out in committees. Both houses of Congress have a number of committees made up of several members from each political party. The chairperson of a committee is usually a member of the majority party who has been on the committee longer than any of the others. This is called the seniority system.

Members of the majority party elect a majority leader, who tries to get that party's bills voted into law. The minority leader tries to get *that* party's bills voted into law.

In each house of Congress, a party whip is also elected by each party. The whip's job is to see that the party's members are present when important votes are taken.

Voting is done in different ways. A bill can be passed by a simple majority vote. This means that more than half of the congresspersons present vote for it. When the bill is very important, the Senate takes a roll-call vote, recording how each senator votes. In the House of Representatives, a voice vote is sometimes used. Those in favor of a proposal say "Aye," and those opposed say "Nay."

The speaker of the House of Representatives announces the results of a voice vote. The speaker is elected by the entire House and is usually the most respected and influential member of the majority party in the House. It is a very important job, because if the President and Vice President were to die or be removed from office, the speaker of the House would become President.

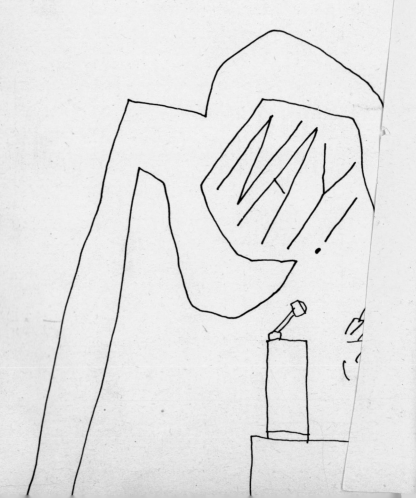

Standing committees, such as the Senate Foreign Relations Committee, are permanent committees. The members of the standing committees may change, but the committee itself goes on.

Subcommittees are made up of part of the membership of a standing committee. A sub-committee investigates specific issues, holds hearings, and makes recommendations to the full committee. The committee then decides what new legislation to propose.

Select committees, or special committees, are established for a limited period of time. They study specific issues, make recommendations for new laws, and are then dissolved.

Joint committees are made up of an equal number of House and Senate members. They study difficult issues over a long period of time.

When the House and Senate pass different versions of the same bill, a conference committee is formed. The conference committee, made up of senators and representatives, tries to work out a bill that is acceptable to both houses.

Congress has other duties besides passing laws. One of the most important is proposing amendments to the Constitution. Congress decides whether to propose the amendment itself or call a constitutional convention, if two thirds of the states request it. Congress then decides if the states should vote on an amendment in state legislatures or at special state conventions.

Another important power of Congress is to conduct investigations on any matter that comes within its powers. These investigations may be conducted by the entire House or Senate but are usually done by committee. A committee can call witnesses and punish any person who does not obey congressional orders.

Congress also reviews the actions and operations of the other branches of government. It can ask department heads to explain how money is being spent and how policy is being made.

Congress also has the power to impeach and try federal officials. An impeachment occurs when the House agrees to bring charges against the official in question. The trial of an impeached official is then held in the Senate.

The Senate must also approve presidential appointments to many government offices. For example, members of the President's Cabinet and of the United States Supreme Court are confirmed by the Senate. The Senate also has the power to approve, or ratify, treaties with foreign countries.

Both houses of Congress meet in the Capitol building in Washington, D.C. The Capitol has offices for representatives and senators and for their assistants. It also contains the House and Senate chambers, which are the large meeting halls where the two houses of Congress hold their sessions.

Congress holds one regular session every year. It usually begins in January and ends in midsummer. But Congress can decide to begin and end its regular session at any time it wishes to. The President may call a special session of Congress after the regular session is ended. A special session is called only when there are issues that are very important and cannot wait for the next regular session to begin.

While the Senate and the House of Representatives usually hold separate sessions, they sometimes meet together in a joint session in the House chamber. Joint sessions may be held when the President or some other important dignitary comes to Congress to make a major speech. For example, the President's "State of the Union" address, given every year, is delivered before a joint session of Congress. No voting or lawmaking takes place at a joint session.

Members of Congress play an important role in American political life. They must propose legislation, attend a wide variety of events, and be present for committee meetings and conferences. They must take part in debates and floor votes. Sometimes they must travel to distant places, in order to gather facts. And they must visit their home districts, to find out what the voters want.

After all, each congressperson—whether senator or representative—was elected by the voters back home. And he or she must serve those voters' best interests—while keeping the national interests in mind as well.

It's a big job—and it's a very important job.